This Moth

By Liza Charlesworth

ISBN: 978-1-339-02772-2

Art Director: Tannaz Fassihi; Designer: Tanya Chernyak
Photos © Getty Images and Shutterstock.com.
Copyright © Liza Charlesworth. All rights reserved. Published by Scholastic Inc.

1 2 3 4 5 6 7 8 9 10   68   32 31 30 29 28 27 26 25 24 23

Printed in Jiaxing, China. First printing, August 2023.

fuzz

leg

wing

A moth is a bug with wings.
It has thick fuzz.
It has six thin legs.

This moth is tan.

That moth has spots.

This moth is big.

It is as big as a bat!

That moth is NOT big.

It is as small as an ant.

This moth sips from a plant.

That moth sits on a thumb.

This moth flaps its wings.

That moth lays eggs
on a plant by a path.

Crack, crack! The eggs hatch.
Then, when it gets hot,
you will spot lots of moths!